Creating Your Re-entry Plan

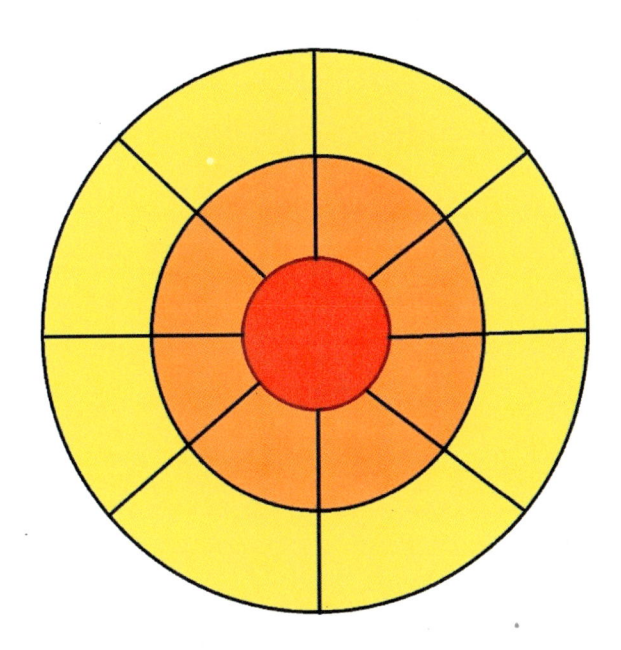

Gatekeepers Business of Living Program

223 N. Prospect St
Hagerstown, MD 21740
www.gatekeepersmd.org
814-574-4354

GATEKEEPERS – CREATING YOUR RE-ENTRY PLAN

Copyright © 2020 Gatekeepers
Updated March 2021
All rights reserved.
ISBN: 9781097883905

Table of Contents

ACKNOWLEDGEMENTS 5

FOREWORD 7

INTRODUCTION 11

CHAPTER ONE – FIRST MINUTES OF FREEDOM 15

CHAPTER TWO – CHALLENGES FOR RETURNING CITIZENS 17

CHAPTER THREE – BASIC NEEDS 19

CHAPTER FOUR – A COMPLETED EXAMPLE BULLSEYE 21

CHAPTER FIVE – BUSINESS OF LIVING OVERVIEW 23

CHAPTER SIX – BUSINESS OF LIVING PLAN WORKSHEET - OCCUPATIONAL 25

CHAPTER SEVEN – BUSINESS OF LIVING PLAN WORKSHEET - EDUCATIONAL 27

CHAPTER EIGHT – BUSINESS OF LIVING PLAN WORKSHEET – PERSONAL 29

CHAPTER NINE – BUSINESS OF LIVING PLAN WORKSHEET - SPIRITUAL 31

CHAPTER TEN – BUSINESS OF LIVING WORKSHEETS 33

CHAPTER ELEVEN – RE-ENTRY CHECKLIST 41

CHAPTER TWELVE – SUCCESS STORIES 45

CHAPTER THIRTEEN – BILL GAERTNER'S BIOGRAPHY 49

APPENDIX A - BUSINESS OF LIVING COACHING AGREEMENT 51

A warm thanks to the Order of Malta, Federal Association for their financial support in helping get this book distributed to as many inmates and ex-offenders around the nation as possible.

ACKNOWLEDGEMENTS

This book has been written for inmates and ex-offenders entirely by ex-offenders who have experienced what it is like to re-enter society after having been incarcerated. The contributors all worked together to develop an approach to help others move forward. It is the product of people coming together over the past six years from all struggles and different walks of life to identify what is essential.

The network of individuals who met and became friends and shared experiences established a network now known as Gatekeepers. The keys to Gatekeepers are its committed volunteers (mostly ex-offenders) and the ability to draw upon community resources to aid those struggling to overcome their past. The Gatekeepers network includes too many to mention as many hundreds of men and women from local, state, and federal penitentiaries and recovery homes have walked through its door. Each of them has provided testimony, wisdom, or support to others in some way often bringing themselves or others to tears. We acknowledge each and every one of us has a force within us to move ourselves or others and to seek to be the very best we can be while searching for meaning and purpose.

A special thanks to Leanne Kuehnle who has worked diligently on all phases of this book and also to Keith Roys who has provided his experience as an author of prison ministry resources to pull all of this together, edit it, revise it multiple times, and get it published!

Also, a special thanks to all of the coaches that Bill Gaertner, the founder of Gatekeepers, has worked with over the years. These folks have instilled in Bill a coaching mentality that, while caring, is direct, no nonsense and demanding of hard work. This coaching approach has become the cornerstone of this Workbook.

FOREWORD

For a number of years, Bill was an outstanding college basketball coach; he used his coaching skills to develop young players and help them grow on and off the court. Now Bill is using his life experiences to help ex-offenders, equipping them to build successful lives.

Gary Williams
Retired NCAA Champion University of Maryland Basketball Coach
Inducted into NAISMITH Basketball Hall of Fame

I played for Coach Gaertner as the senior captain at Norwich University. It was the first time I heard about the Business of Living. It greatly helped form my plan for living a fulfilling professional and personal life. I was a successful high school coach in Haverhill, Massachusetts and moved on to be Principal by the age of 31 and then Superintendent of Schools. The title I most revered was 'coach'. I never forgot the leadership lessons and his simple plan for success! I am retired in Florida and after 50 years I still call him coach.

Scott Williams
St Augustine, Florida

Although Bill was with us at the University of Connecticut as an Assistant Coach for just a year, he continued his coaching career at several other universities for a number of years. Bill always had a heart to work with people from all kinds of skills and backgrounds. Now he does this, working with ex-offenders, as well as anyone I know.

Dee Rowe
Retired Head Basketball Coach, UCONN
Inducted into NAISMITH Basketball Hall of Fame

Gatekeepers now provides reentering inmates with a clearinghouse of services available, the Day Report Center participants with practical knowledge, and the Adult Drug Court participants with a mentor. As judge for the Washington County Adult Drug Court, I have come to understand the necessity to provide therapeutic, occupational, educational, personal and spiritual growth opportunities for the participants.

Brett R. Wilson
Former Maryland State Delegate

You and your team work with those involved with the criminal justice system so they are better equipped to successfully transition back into society. This includes peer support, enhancing interpersonal skills, job training, acquiring gainful employment, and on-going mentoring.

Paul Frey
President & CEO, Washington County, MD Chamber of Commerce

Gatekeepers has been a vital partner in the re-entry of offenders both at the local and state levels. Gatekeepers provides valuable programs and support to the Day Reporting Center.

Sheriff Doug Mullendore
Washington County, MD Sheriff's Office

I am familiar with Gatekeepers and its successes in building a premier re-entry program in Washington County, Maryland, that includes specifically a unique ability to successfully gather all various programs to work together in unison.

Rebecca R. Hogamier
Program Director, Washington County, MD Sheriff's Office, Day Reporting Center

Gatekeepers has played an integral role in the success of many individuals being reconnected to their communities by assisting them with life-coaching skills, and by providing necessities such as transportation, employment, clothing, and housing to give them a sense of purpose and reconnection.

U.S. District Judge Alexander Williams, Jr. (ret)
UMD College of Behavioral & Social Sciences

Through our partnership with Gatekeepers, we are seeing tremendous success with individuals who successfully have re-entered society, established healthy relationships, taken responsibility for their financial obligations, paying taxes, and contributing to the betterment of society. Gatekeepers is an organization that we have fully embraced as a partner because of our shared re-entry vision. We believe that lives are changed one life at a time when we work together to provide the individual with a healthy, safe, and accountable environment.

Clarence Horst
President of the Board, Celebration Ministries, Hagerstown, MD

Over the last three years, the Business of Living and Resource Club meetings provided by Gatekeepers has enhanced the lives of many women in various stages of their recovery. These meetings have been instrumental in helping the women find the required tools and peer support necessary for a successful reentry and a life never imagined!

Kylie Johnson
CEO, Lasting Change Women's Recovery House, Hagerstown, MD

Gatekeepers' mission to serve incarcerated men and women and ex-offenders, those human beings society has ignored, is a beacon of hope in the goodness of humankind. As a member of the Order of Malta's North American Prison Ministry Apostolate, the Apostolate and I have been blessed to work with, and support, Bill Gaertner and Gatekeepers almost from its inception. I know first-hand that Gatekeepers has helped hundreds of men and women inside and outside of prison to improve their lives as productive, hardworking citizens.

This Workbook is just one example of Gatekeepers' outreach. It is designed to prepare those in prison for a smoother re-entry and to encourage them, and ex-offenders, to continue their growth journey with Gatekeepers upon release. What a wonderful opportunity for this important group of men and women who we encourage to take advantage of this material.

Mike McGarry
Co-chair, Order of Malta's North American Prison Ministry Apostolate

INTRODUCTION

> *A personal message from Bill Gaertner, Founder and Executive Director of Gatekeepers, about how to use this book in order to run the successful **Business of Living** of YOUR life.*

I would like to begin with two important aspects of this workbook: (1) why we wrote it and (2) why we use a coaching approach.

(1) This book and the vision to start Gatekeepers originated on the recreation yard of the Metropolitan Transition Center in Baltimore, MD, in 2010. That is when I met Keith Roys and we started speaking about re-entry and our lives after release. We shared common backgrounds, education, and spiritual feelings (key components in the **Business of Living Program**). Keith has written over a dozen prison ministry books since being released in 2012 and volunteers with Gatekeepers. Keith and I realized there was no structured re-entry planning for inmates and little for those released. We decided to work to fix that. We, along with dozens of other ex-offenders, spent months talking and gathering information used in developing this book just for you.

(2) As my biography at the back of the book explains, prior to founding Gatekeepers and prior to my incarceration, I was a college basketball player as well as an assistant and head basketball coach at a number of colleges. As an ex-offender I have found that inmates and ex-offenders (men and women) relate well to the coaching skills I have developed. This Workbook builds on these coaching skills- it is direct, provides the necessary information without a lot of fanfare and most importantly, demands individual responsibility in developing personal re-entry (LIFE) plans.

A coach's job is to convince players (YOU) to do the hard things that they (YOU) don't want to do in order to be who they (YOU) want to be. So, let me be clear, using this Workbook you can develop a LIFE plan and take major steps in making that plan a reality. It will require hard work on your part, but remember, you will have a coach on your back, pushing you to make you who you can be.

For you who are incarcerated, we are giving this to you now, while incarcerated, because your re-entry planning starts the first day of your incarceration! We will work with you while you are inside and continue to work with you once you walk out of prison. For you who have been released, this Workbook and its Business of Living Program can be your way to a more meaningful life.

This book is a workplan for you to think about you. It is structured to identify what will be a challenge for you and to coach you on what you need to do to help you move forward. Our

Business of Living approach is designed to help you identify and overcome any challenges you may face focusing on four aspects of living your life – occupational, educational, personal, and spiritual. It is our belief that when you do things from your soul, you will feel joy.

I welcome you to consider the following "Four Agreements" while taking this journey with us, using this workbook to prepare your own re-entry plan. The Four Agreements[1] are:

1. Be true to your word;
2. Don't take anything personally;
3. Don't make assumptions; and
4. Always do your best.

Now let's work together to identify and reach your goals. We will begin with an overview of the Workbook.

Chapter One provides a glimpse of what a person faces when being released from prison and asks you what choices you might make differently from the (true) story provided. **Chapter Two** presents a lot of the challenges you will face when returning to society that you should think about because you too may face many of them. **Chapter Three** focuses on Dr. Maslow's respected "triangle" that orders our needs from most basic (bottom of the triangle) to achieving of life goals (top of the triangle). This Chapter presents some background information on every person's basic needs to survive realizing we all start again at the bottom and must work hard to move up to the top of the triangle. **Chapter Four** provides a completed Bullseye (your Life Plan!) meant to show you what you are shooting for. This Life Plan, this Bullseye, places you in the red section, with orange being the resources that can help you move to the yellow part which are your life goals. You will fill out this Bullseye based on what you learn and do in the following chapters. This will become your Life Plan. **Chapter Five** introduces you to the **Business of Living Program** providing an overview of the four fundamental program areas (Occupational, Educational, Personal, and Spiritual). **Chapters Six, Seven, Eight and Nine** deal with each of these four program areas which we refer to as the four PILLARS (that hold up your house-YOU). By taking one pillar at a time, we break the Bullseye into four sections. We will ask questions to make you think about what should be included in your own Bullseye, your own Life Plan. It is important that you take notes on the blank sheets provided because at the end of each of these four chapters you will fill out one quarter of the Bullseye. Consider each program area, each pillar, as two pieces of your pie on the Bullseye. Once you have completed each of the four program areas, your pie should be whole.

Please keep in mind that although we get released from incarceration, we are still in the middle of the circle, in the red; we are the target. We must work to move out to the yellow, our goals, where we want to be. We cannot get to the yellow without going through the orange. The orange section is our posse, the folks who care about us and/or can help us to reach the things we really want in life. Your coach will provide you with information about available resources that you will need. Some prisons and jails provide resource guides, as do some States, counties, and Parole and Probation Offices.

Chapter Ten provides some blank Bullseyes for your use. **Chapter Eleven** provides a re-entry checklist of necessary tasks and associated community resources to help you. Your coach can help you complete your identified needs. **Chapter Twelve** presents some success stories from Gatekeepers Graduates. **Appendix A** is the **Business of Living** coaching agreement that you will need to read and sign before you start the **Business of Living Program**.

In closing, if you are incarcerated or just released and need any re-entry information please call or write to me at:

Gatekeepers
223 North Prospect Street
Hagerstown, MD 21740
814-574-4354

All the best to you!

Bill

---

[1] Ruiz, Miguel, and Janet Mills. *The Four Agreements: A Practical Guide to Personal Freedom*, 1997. Print.

ASAP = Always Stop And Pray!

CHAPTER ONE – FIRST MINUTES OF FREEDOM

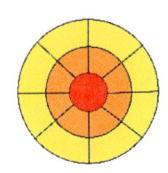

Getting released from prison can be one of the happiest moments for some. But that joy can fade quickly when the realities of life in the free world take hold. The reality is that most have great fear about facing the world— and failure—once again. $50 in cash is what you're handed when you're released from prison. You walk out at 5pm and look around. Not much seems different—hopefully it's different enough to keep you from a repeat performance.

You head toward your aunt's house. It's the address you gave Case Management. Most of your family and friends rejected you after hearing about this "trip" to prison, but you hope she will let you stay a few nights. As you walk the streets and ride the bus, you see familiar faces from your past—drug users, dealers and prostitutes—you are immediately confronted with temptation. You might even be offered the opportunity to make a deal that will increase your start-up funding by at least tenfold: just sell a little crack.

You get to your aunt's house at 7pm only to find out she will not let you stay the night, or any night. She makes you a sandwich and sends you away. You throw your laundry bag containing your prison possessions (a few changes of underwear, socks, and t-shirts and maybe a fan and some shower shoes) over your shoulder and leave.

You're hungry, but money is tight. The dollar menu at McDonalds is your lean cuisine—$45 left.

It's getting dark. You look around for a place to sleep for the night and find some bushes and trees in the nearby park that you think you can crawl into and not be seen by the cops. It's summer time and it won't get too cold at night and it doesn't look like it is going to rain.

An ambulance siren wakes you at 5:00 a.m. It's the next morning, time for your first parole visit … can't be late or you'll get revoked. You're not familiar with the bus system and it takes you 30 minutes to plan your route. One wrong move will cost you time, money, and maybe your freedom. Four dollars, five busses and three hours later, you arrive at the parole office just in time. You anxiously wait for two hours before you are called in to see your parole officer. She is straightforward and firm about the rules and expectations she has of you. She also tells you that you can write a letter to your judge requesting a waiver of your probation and parole fees.

It's past lunch by the time you leave parole. You are starving. McDonalds again. $36 left. You use the McDonalds bathroom to clean up a little bit. You search the neighborhood for a thrift store. No one will hire you if you are wearing the ill-fitting clothes you wore walking out of prison. You find dress pants, a shirt, a tie and a pair of shoes at the local thrift store for $15. $21 left.

You are dedicated enough to find a local unemployment center that offers computers to start your job search. Tomorrow you will hit the streets and fill out applications after you apply for food stamps. You need to find a place to live too. No address = possible parole violation = bad. No dinner tonight, need to conserve money. You head back to the park for the night.

The next day is a total waste. You spend another $4 in bus fares ($17 left) and 12 hours in line at the Food Stamp office, and you walk away empty-handed. If only you would have known to arrive when the line started forming at 4:00 a.m. No food stamps, no job, but you need some food and get a loaf of bread and jar of peanut butter. $13 left.

Morale is taking a nose-dive as you head back to the park again. You have one clean set of underwear and socks left.

The rejection you receive job-searching the next day is brutal. The bus rides costs money ($9 left) and time, and HR people do not take kindly to felons. One office even escorted you out with security guards. You have been out four days, and you're not even close to a job lead. Hunger strikes again and all you can get is a candy bar. $8 left.

At the bus stop on the way back to the park, a shady character offers a deal that is hard to refuse. You're an expert at selling dope. Go forward with your $8 or revert to a life of fast money?

Which would you choose?

_____

_____

_____

_____

CHAPTER TWO – CHALLENGES FOR RETURNING CITIZENS

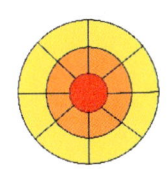

Many inmates have been in prison more than once and some even boast about it. However, for some inmates, their goal is to own their own business or they have a brother or cousin who has a home improvement business and a job and a place for them to stay once they get out. Realistically, most inmates are totally unprepared for release. Some are so scared they may commit an infraction that will delay their release date, making their future even more uncertain except for one certainty...MORE TIME!

Some specific challenges faced by inmates about to be released include:

- No realistic home plan
- No safe lodging
- Limited relationship with God
- Mental health issues
- Lack of reliable transportation
- Short-term optimistic outlook
- Lack of career skills
- Child support, including arrearages
- "I Got It" attitude
- No career focus
- Only $50
- No ID
- Addicted to meds, alcohol, other things
- Job interviews with a criminal record
- No high school diploma or GED
- Debts
- Limited respect for authority
- No support group
- No cell phone
- Only prison clothing
- Reconnecting with family and friends

Which of these do you feel like will be challenges for you? What other issues will be a challenge for you?

_____
_____
_____
_____
_____
_____
_____
_____
_____
_____
_____
_____
_____
_____

This workbook will help you identify and deal with these challenges as you prepare for your re-entry!

CHAPTER THREE – BASIC NEEDS

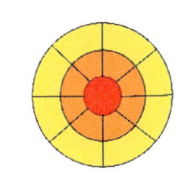

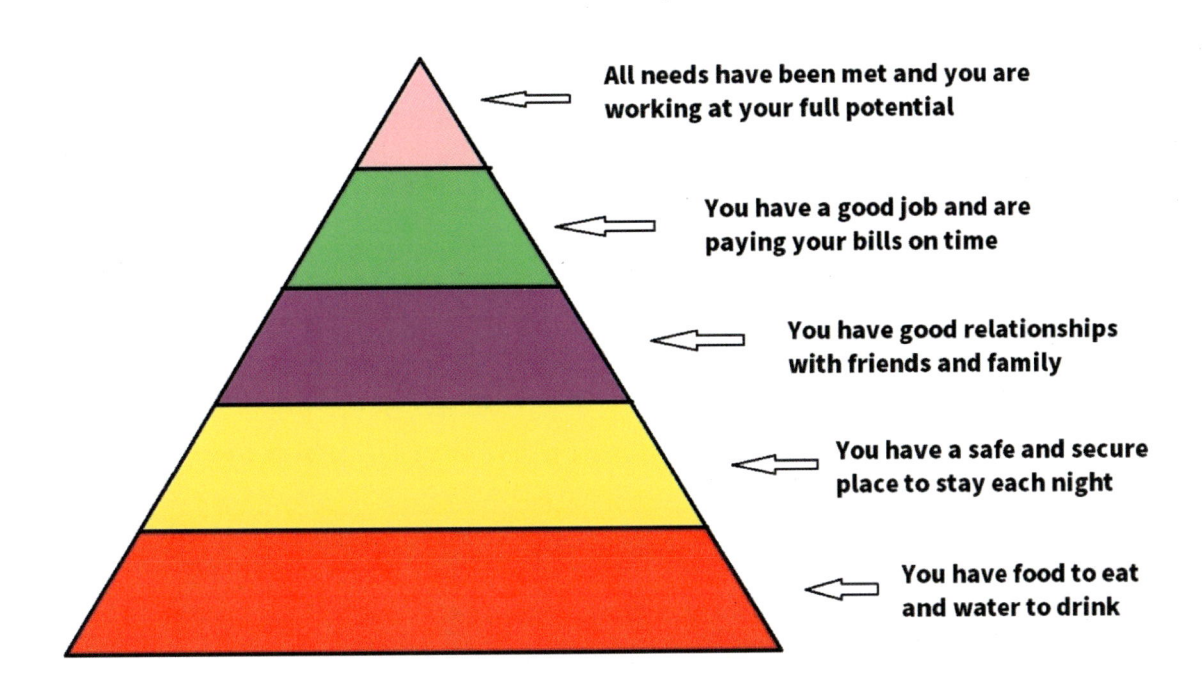

- All needs have been met and you are working at your full potential
- You have a good job and are paying your bills on time
- You have good relationships with friends and family
- You have a safe and secure place to stay each night
- You have food to eat and water to drink

Abraham Maslow, a psychologist, wrote a paper in 1943 proposing the theory that everyone has basic needs that must be taken care of (starting at the bottom layer of the diagram above) before a person could really start moving up to the next layer. As a person moves up layer after layer, they would, in theory, become more confident and successful.

When you look at the re-entry process, using Maslow's theory, you can see it makes sense because having a reliable source of food and safe shelter gives a person a sense of stability so they can then start to work on building relationships and finding a good job.

This workbook will help you look at all of these needs and make sure they get worked into your re-entry plan.

A goal without a plan is just a wish!

GATEKEEPERS – CREATING YOUR RE-ENTRY PLAN

CHAPTER FOUR – A COMPLETED EXAMPLE BULLSEYE

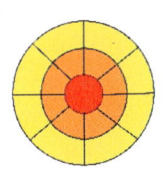

We provide a completed Bullseye upfront to let you see what a Life plan looks like. As mentioned in the overview, the red is YOU and the yellow are your goals. The orange are the resources you need to draw on the reach the yellow. This may seem too simple, but hundreds of folks have successfully completed this program using the Bullseye and they really like it, it becomes part of them-their road map to a new life.

Leanne

Inner ring (orange resources): Celebrate Recovery 12 step program; Gatekeepers; Church family; Family; Friends; Hagerstown Community College; Close clean friends; Rehab & mental health counsel

Outer ring (yellow goals): Forgiveness of self and others; Living each day to its fullest; Completely surrendered to God; Caring relationship with family; Helping others each and every day; Career in real estate; Acceptance of my current life; Sober

Turn your "cant's" into "cans" and your dreams into plans!

CHAPTER FIVE – BUSINESS OF LIVING OVERVIEW

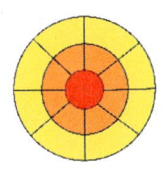

The *Business of Living* works to motivate, empower, and encourage ex-offenders.

Gatekeepers' approaches re-entry from a unique and compassionate perspective called the **Business of Living**. This program is designed to help you identify and overcome those challenges to re-entry that might prevent you from being who you want to be. You have to accept the challenge for your own self-learning and be brave enough to make some necessary changes to the way you have been thinking and living. The **Business of Living** process will focus on four areas: occupational, educational, personal, and spiritual aspects of your life. It is important that you understand that these four areas, PILLARS, are intertwined-you need to work on all four of the areas for a successful life. Gatekeepers' **Business of Living** provides mentoring that builds on the concept that when you do things from your soul, you will feel joy.

The coaching and information we provide is designed to help you move forward to be your best. We help you prepare your personal re-entry plan and what you should do in order to run the successful **Business of Living** of YOUR life!

Occupational
- A job/occupation/career provides purpose, responsibility, and accountability
- You must develop the skills that are needed for what your goal is
- There must be a match between your ability and the occupation you desire
- Market yourself positively

Educational
- Identify your current educational level
- What educational level do you want to attain
- What do you need to reach your educational goal (personal and/or work-related)
- Assess your current skill set
- Complete the training/classes you need to reach your goal

Personal
- Remove any obstacles that are holding you back:
  - Substance Abuse
  - Anger Management
  - Housing/Transportation
  - Stress Management

  Re-establish relationships
  Money management
  Forgive yourself and others

Spiritual
- What does spirituality mean to you
- Do you have a religious background
- What are your goals for a spiritual life
- Do you have an accountability partner
- The spirit within:
  - guides each of us to strive for meaning and purpose in our lives
  - guides our greatest dreams and accompanies our darkest moments
  - inspires us to seek the very best which we are capable
  - is the inspiration of all that is joyful in each of us

On the following pages we will discuss each of these four key areas in more detail to help you make some decisions on the actions you need to take in each area as you prepare your re-entry plan, as you prepare your life plan.

Gatekeepers' coaches are going to challenge you to make positive choices that will help you have a successful transition back into the community. In Appendix A, you will find the **Business of Living** Coaching Agreement. It spells out both the Gatekeepers Values and Expectations and the **Business of Living Program** Commitments. You need to read through and sign the Coaching Agreement before you start the **Business of Living Program**.

CHAPTER SIX – BUSINESS OF LIVING PLAN WORKSHEET - OCCUPATIONAL

A career provides purpose, responsibility, and accountability. Anyone can get a job, but it takes a focused person to develop a career. You must develop the skills that are needed for what your career goals are. You have to be realistic: your abilities need to match the career you desire. However, with training and education you could become a warehouse worker, an electrician, an executive chef, a commercial driver, or a business owner!

- What does your current resume look like (list job titles, start/stop dates, job tasks)?

_____
_____
_____

- What career fields interest you (example: I want to become an electrician)?

_____
_____
_____

- What training, skills, and abilities do you need for the career you want (example: I need to get an apprenticeship as a journeyman electrician)?

_____
_____
_____

- What steps do I need to take to get the training I need (example: sign up for courses at the local community college)?

_____
_____
_____

GATEKEEPERS – CREATING YOUR RE-ENTRY PLAN

- The things that could interfere with my plans, and how I will deal with them, are (example: old habits – find new friends that will support and encourage me):

_____

_____

_____

Now, as shown on the example Bullseye on page 21, put your Occupational data in your Bullseye here.

CHAPTER SEVEN – BUSINESS OF LIVING PLAN WORKSHEET - EDUCATIONAL

Completing additional education develops time management skills, perseverance to attain goals, commitment, and fosters relationships. Attaining a degree or certificate proves your abilities to yourself and others.

- What is the highest level of education you have right now (GED/high school diploma, tech school, college degree, graduate degree)?

  _____
  _____
  _____

- What current skills or certifications do you have (list them all!)?

  _____
  _____
  _____

- What educational level do you want to attain?

  _____
  _____
  _____

- What do you need to reach your educational goals?

  _____
  _____
  _____

Now, as shown on the example Bullseye on Page 21, put your Educational data in your Bullseye here.

CHAPTER EIGHT – BUSINESS OF LIVING PLAN WORKSHEET – PERSONAL

Being honest with yourself about your personal issues is important. You need to see how they may have contributed to your past problems and find ways to resolve and overcome them.

- What existing mental health or past trauma issues do you have?

  _____
  _____
  _____

- What health issues do you have?

  _____
  _____
  _____

- Are you eating properly and exercising?

  _____
  _____
  _____

- What actions do you need take to be as presentable as you can (for example: fix your teeth, lose some weight, pay attention to your personal grooming, get good clothes)

  _____
  _____
  _____

- Are you good with your finances? (example: pay bills on time, have a budget)

  _____
  _____
  _____

GATEKEEPERS – CREATING YOUR RE-ENTRY PLAN

- What does a model good citizen look like to you? (volunteer, vote, jury duty)
_____
_____
_____

- Are you ready to commit to obeying rules and laws?
_____
_____
_____

Now, as shown on the example Bullseye on Page 21, put your Personal data in your Bullseye here.

CHAPTER NINE – BUSINESS OF LIVING PLAN WORKSHEET - SPIRITUAL

The spirit within guides each of us to strive for meaning and purpose in our lives. The spirit guides our greatest dreams and is with us in our darkest moments. It inspires us to be the very best of which we are capable. The spirit is the inspiration of ***all that is joyful*** in each of us.

- What does spirituality mean to you?

  _____
  _____
  _____

- Do you have a religious background?

  _____
  _____
  _____

- What are your goals for a spiritual life?

  _____
  _____
  _____

- Do you have an accountability partner?

  _____
  _____
  _____

- The changes I want to make in my spiritual life are (example: read the Bible, go to a church service, talk to a spiritual leader/mentor):

_____
_____
_____

Now, as shown on the example Bullseye on Page 21, put your Spiritual data in your Bullseye here.

CHAPTER TEN – BUSINESS OF LIVING WORKSHEETS

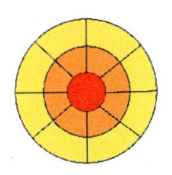

You will be preparing your own personal Bullseye chart over the next few pages. We have provided two rough draft blanks for you to use and one for your final plan.

Do not judge other people whose sins are different than yours!

GATEKEEPERS – CREATING YOUR RE-ENTRY PLAN

Your Personal **Business of Living** Worksheet (rough draft #1)

Now copy all of the data you entered on pages 26, 28, 30, and 32 to the Bullseye here.

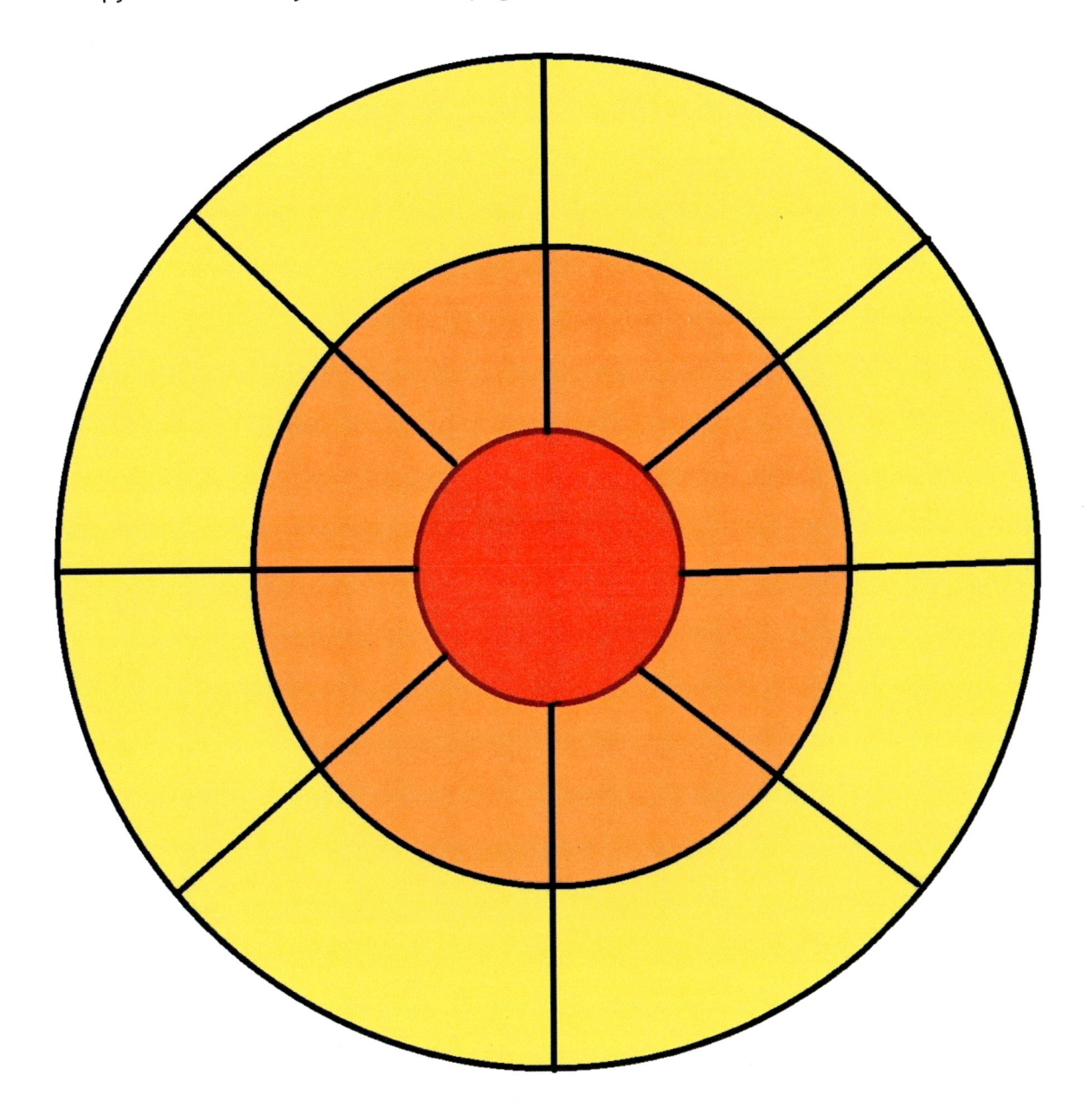

Complaining opens the door to self-pity and anger!

Your Personal **Business of Living** Worksheet (rough draft #2)

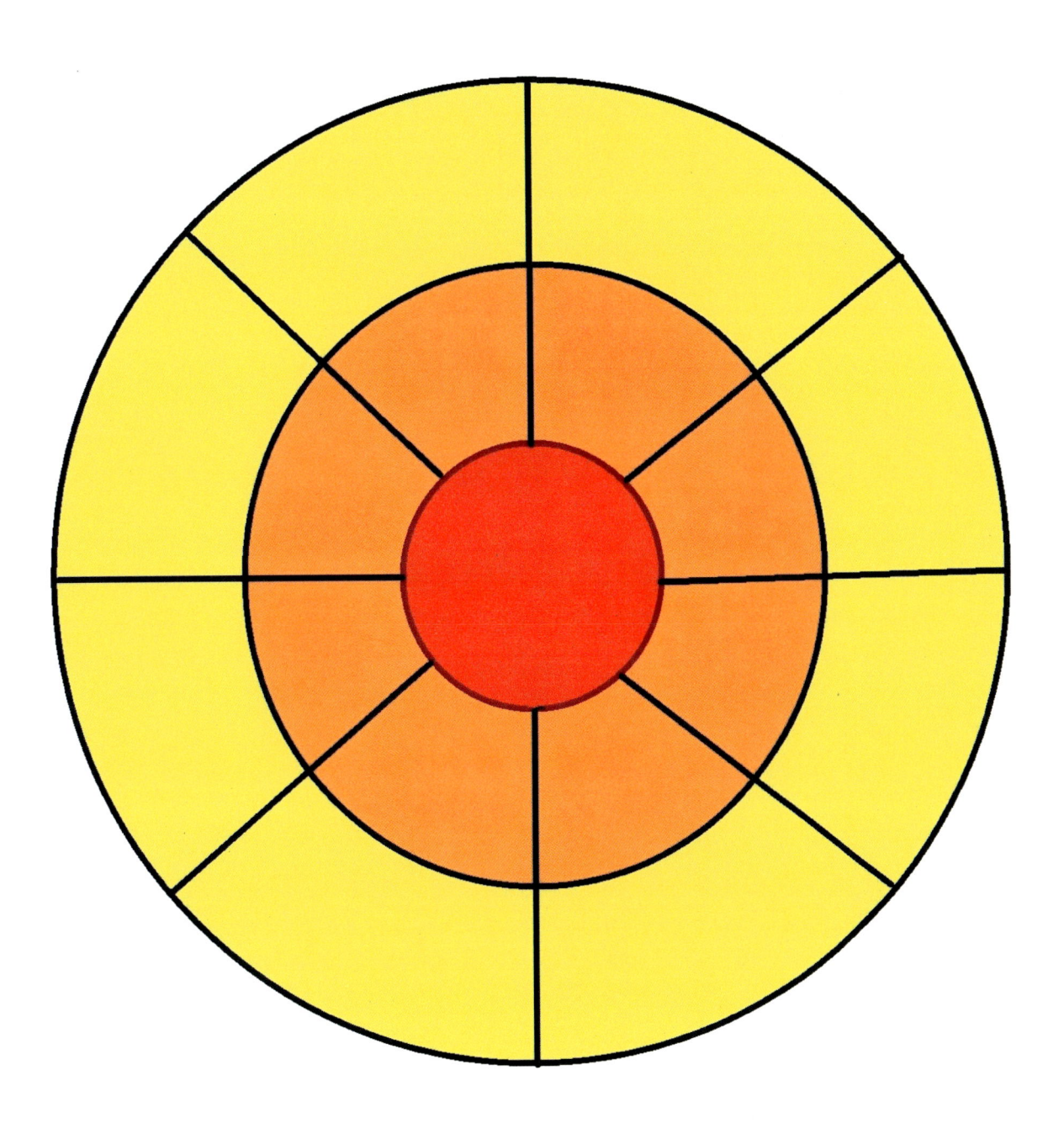

We are born to make mistakes, not to fake perfection

Your Personal **Business of Living** Worksheet (final)

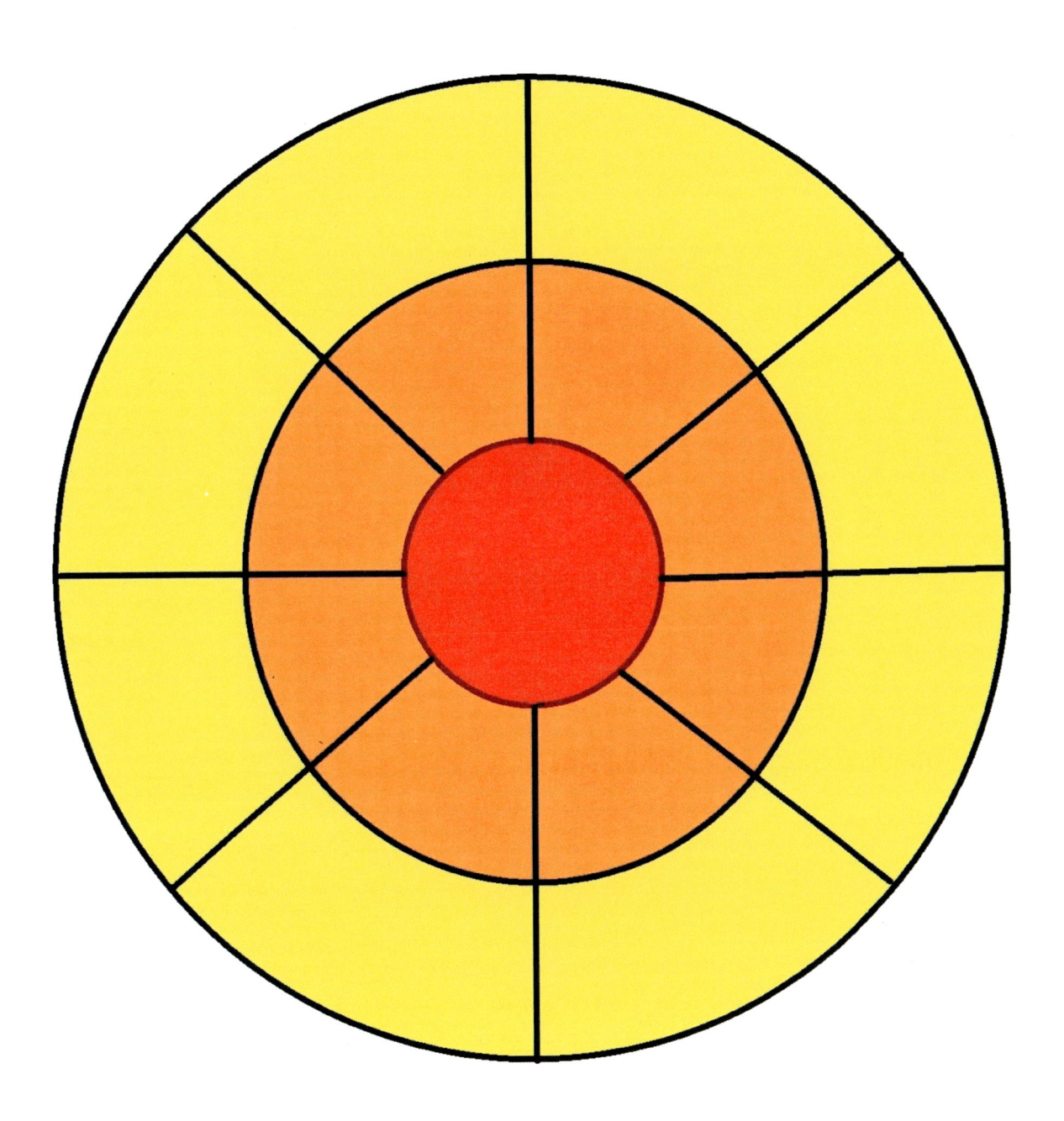

If you fail to plan, you plan to fail!

CHAPTER ELEVEN – RE-ENTRY CHECKLIST

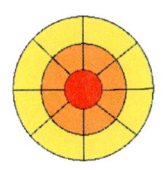

The checklist on the following page has a lot of the common things everyone needs to consider and, as needed, make a part of their personal re-entry plan. Take the actions items you developed in the Occupational, Educational, Personal, and Spiritual sections and add them to the bottom of the checklist in the blank rows.

If incarcerated, you can get started on some items right now, some you can complete, and some you will start and complete after your release. For ex-offenders there is nothing holding you back from working on these items right now. In either case, we will work with you while inside to prepare, review, and finalize your checklist….YOUR re-entry plan!

We will also help in implementing all of your actions.

Once you complete all of the actions, you'll be a Gatekeepers **Business of Living** Graduate!

Is this another 'One Day' or is this 'Day One' of your new life....you decide!

GATEKEEPERS

For the gate is narrow and the way is hard that leads to LIFE.
Matthew 7:14

CREATING YOUR RE-ENTRY PLAN

Tasks (as applicable)	Name	Contact Number
Plan the first 24 hours (who will pick you up, where will you sleep, etc.)		
Schedule and attend initial Parole & Probation meeting		
Get proper identification (Birth Certificate, Social Security Card, Driver's License, State ID card, etc.)		
Get safe housing		
Get clothing (job and everyday)		
Food – sign up for SNAP, locate free food services around town		
Transportation – bus passes are available if you don't have access to a car		
Prepare to pay child support		
Employment: resume prep, interview prep, set up interviews		
Sign up for health care		
Sign up for Veterans assistance		
Get a cell phone		
Get help for alcohol or drug abuse issues		
Take care of mental health needs		
Take care of health and dental needs		
Get more training or education		
Prepare to be a parent		
Get connected to a caring community		
Get assistance regarding domestic violence		
Clean up your record and get legal help if needed		
Learn to spend/budget money wisely		
Register to vote		

GATEKEEPERS – CREATING YOUR RE-ENTRY PLAN

Tasks (as applicable)	Name	Contact Number

CHAPTER TWELVE – SUCCESS STORIES

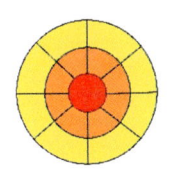

Ollie's Story:
Ollie has been shot, and he has been stabbed. He spent five years in Maryland House of Corrections and ten years at Maryland Corrections Training Center. His mom passed away and his dad was put into a care facility in another state while he was in prison. Ollie found that changes occurred when he finally began to pray. His negativity flipped, and he lost all of his bad habits in prison. While incarcerated Ollie completed his GED, took some college credits and worked for Maryland Correction Enterprises. Ollie saw that the majority of those he knew who were about to be released or who were recently released were looking for a handout. Ollie was looking for tools, keeping his faith, and willing to work for it. Ollie wanted it! Ollie began working as a painter after release. He networked and has worked in the logistics area for the past few years. He now owns his own house, has a new car, and has re-established relationships with his family. Ollie recognizes the need to help other people. That's what Gatekeepers' mission is all about. Ollie told us that "Gatekeepers gives people a better chance and encouragement."

Steve's Story:
Steve was incarcerated for five years in the State of Maryland. Upon release in Baltimore City, MD, he was released to a halfway house and got a Pell Grant to Stratford Culinary Institute. Steve spent hours each day for years riding public transportation to complete his studies – an effort few would have endured. He got his first job working with an extraordinary chef and later became General Manager/Chef for an international culinary program based in Baltimore. Currently, Steve is the Head Chef for the Franciscan Center in Baltimore, MD, feeding 500 people each day. He gives testimony and speeches to many returning citizens in the state of Maryland and is inspirational with his smile! He gives speeches throughout the State of Maryland and on network television about the importance of faith and food.

Grady's Story:
Grady came to Gatekeepers from the Wells House program. In very short period of time, he became a regular participant in the Resource Clubs and without an ID, was able to get a full-time job with a local employer. He has been promoted several times already. As a result, he was able to get his own apartment, a savings account in a local bank, and he has been in Gatekeeper's videos. He is now a peer coach and role model for others just beginning their re-entry journey.

Mark's Story:
Mark was incarcerated over 20 years among federal and state penitentiaries and released to Hagerstown, MD, two years ago. He immediately became an integral part of the Gatekeepers Business of Living Program and became employed by a local major logistics company. He then started his own transportation business which led to his current business venture as owner of a Carmen's downtown convenience store in Hagerstown, MD. He spends his free time speaking and testifying to various local and state governments in an effort to bring awareness for re-entry obstacles. Mark has received much acclaim from local, state, and national political figures.

Jennifer's Story:
Jennifer had been incarcerated in the Maryland Correctional Institute for Women (MCI-W) in Jessup, MD. Upon release in Hagerstown, she began working in retail and then began volunteering for some non-profits, including Gatekeepers, where she networked. She then began volunteering at Habitat for Humanity and through that organization was able to purchase her own home. At the same time, she successfully established her own cleaning business and became even more involved with Gatekeepers as a peer mentor. She represents herself and Gatekeepers as a speaker for local civic clubs and Lasting Change Recovery House for Women. She also became a member or the Sunrise Rotary Club. Jennifer inspires many others by demonstrating what one can achieve with hard work including the ability to change your life.

Howard's Story:
Howard was incarcerated on and off for 30 years in most prisons throughout Maryland. Upon release he worked for Horizon/Goodwill and at one point was honored as Employee of the Year. Howard volunteered at Lasting Change Recovery Center, Gatekeepers, and Celebrate Recovery. He currently spends most of his time working full time for STAR Foundation aiding senior citizens. He now rents his own apartment and has his own car. He has been an outstanding peer mentor for Gatekeepers for the past six years (since day one) as well as a citizen who exercises his right to vote and responsibly pays taxes.

Joe's Story:
Joe was incarcerated for two different sentences at MD State Penitentiaries for approximately nine years. Upon release he immediately worked several warehouse jobs in Washington and Franklin Counties. He owns a home with his wife and three children and is currently a supervisor for a medical industry service company. Joe spends his free time attending to his family, church, and shooting hoops. He was a highly sought high school basketball recruit years ago and is currently using those skills in ways to help others leaving incarceration and to prevent youth from going down that path. Joe is currently planning to open his own transportation company.

Chris's Story:
Chris was released from prison six years ago having served eight years in the Maryland Department of Corrections. He served several sentences, was sent to Gatekeepers, and immediately was given a job at Horizon/Goodwill in Hagerstown. At the same time, he got a side job painting apartments for a friend of Gatekeepers. Soon after, the people who owned the apartments rented one to him. At that time, he was introduced to a local plumber who hired him as an apprentice and soon after became a full-time plumber. Chris attended Celebrate Recovery through Gatekeepers and long story short, reconnected with his high school sweetheart of many years ago. They married, own a home, and Chris has a fulfilling career with the same plumbing company. Chris told us that, "If it weren't for Gatekeepers, I don't what my story would be. "

Leanne's Story:
Leanne is a very accomplished electrical engineer in the power industry who worked for the federal government for over 25 years. She had an addiction to alcohol that put her in county jail and subsequently with an inexpungible felony. She could no longer go back to her previous employment nor life working with executive government agencies and power utilities and had to start her life over at 54 years old. She was broken (broken hearted; financially distraught; abandoned by her family; and in complete disbelief). After months of volunteering at Gatekeepers providing her testimony and assisting others by using her skills, abilities, and experiences, she found hope and encouragement by studying and embracing the **Business of Living** philosophy. Because of her new found joy and contentment, she has been redirected and is working toward a new career in real estate and is a dedicated Gatekeepers mentor. Leanne lives each day embracing the Four Agreements.

Bob's Story:
Bob was incarcerated for 21 years (RCI, MCTC, WCI, etc.) in the Maryland Department of Corrections. Upon release in Hagerstown, MD, Bob immediately transitioned into Celebrate Recovery Housing. He is a Purple Heart Veteran and spent three months in a rehabilitation program at the Veterans Administration Hospital in Martinsburg, West Virginia. Within the first month of being released, he got his driver's license, purchased a vehicle, and immediately put it to good use as a peer mentor and volunteer at Gatekeepers, Lasting Change, Celebrate Recovery and their associated Saturday pancake breakfast club. Bob's mantra is that he is "Living a life never imagined" while embracing his own **Business of Living**. Bob is about to purchase his own home. Bob represents Disabled American Veterans, VFW, and American Legions around town as well as at the celebrated Memorial Day event in Hagerstown, MD.

Deborah's Story:
Deborah was addicted to drugs and incarcerated on and off spending time in Southern Maryland Detention Centers. She completed the Women's Lasting Change rehabilitation program and while there, became a part-time administrative assistant at Gatekeepers.

Deborah went from Lasting Change to renting her own apartment and working full time as a drug counselor at Awakenings Rehabilitation Program in Hagerstown, MD. Deborah purchased a car and has been clean for two years while working to enhance the lives of others each day.

Wayde's Story:
Wayde spent more than six years in prison. A judge involved in his case referred him to Gatekeepers as he was preparing to be released. Wayde said Gatekeepers among others (including Celebrate Recovery and Mr. Campher, the Washington County Re-Entry Program Coordinator) helped him find his footing. He is working, attending college classes, and building on Gatekeepers' version of the **Business of Living**. Wayde referred to Gatekeepers by saying, "It's community. It's family. And it's a safe place."

Frank's Story:
Frank was in and out of prison his whole life since 18. Prison felt like a second home. It was where he watched Correctional Officers begin their careers and receive several promotions during his times there. When Frank lost someone he loved most dearly, he hit bottom and then nothing mattered. Frank went down a path where he felt nothing inside because he didn't want to feel the pain. While immersed in this pain and desperation he realized that he had the wrong Higher Power. He became aware that this pain was needed in order to heal. Frank sought healing. He got into 'healing programs' and then Drug Court and ultimately released to start over again. Frank started attending Gatekeepers and described how he saw ex-offenders in such a different way than previously. These same individuals who he saw in prison and at the parole and probation office were now offering so much of themselves to others at the weekly Gatekeepers Resource meetings. Frank now has his own apartment and car and has fixed many previously broken relationships. He says he is "Blessed." Frank emphasizes that it doesn't matter whether someone was locked up for six months or 25 years, the world has changed significantly and you need to be prepared as best you can before you get released. Achieve and attain what you can because what you knew and what existed prior to you being incarcerated is not the same now.

CHAPTER THIRTEEN – BILL GAERTNER'S BIOGRAPHY

Bill Gaertner is at work on two sides of restorative justice in Maryland. Gaertner is the founder and leader of Gatekeepers in Washington County, a program that helps ex-offenders transition back into their communities after serving time in prison.

How does he know what they need? He's been in their shoes. Gaertner served eight-and-a-half years in prison for domestic abuse. In fact, he didn't get off probation until September 2020.

The story of his own search for redemption would sound familiar to a Catholic audience. A Catholic deacon at the Metropolitan Transition Center gave me Henri Nouwen's Book, *The Return of the Prodigal Son*, based on Rembrandt's painting. It became his Bible. He still carries it around with me wherever he goes. It was the foundation for his re-entry program. He got out Sept. 23, 2013, and six days later went to St. Mary's in Hagerstown. He walked into the 9:30 Mass and there was a life-sized painting of the Prodigal Son. He cried and knew then that this was where he belonged. That is how Gatekeepers started (in 2014). It is all based on the Prodigal Son.

Gatekeepers operates out of a sparse office in Hagerstown and runs on a "keep-it-simple" philosophy. One of its most valuable tools is a one-page checklist that helps ex-offenders navigate their return to the community. The No. 1 task? Being responsible by reporting to probation/parole, as required. But the sheet of paper is more than a to-do list. Gaertner also has worked with agencies and nonprofit organizations so he knows where to direct people who need clothes, a place to stay, or a hand in finding work.

Those who come through the Gatekeepers door also find they have to take responsibility for themselves. They learn, or re-learn, basic job readiness, job skills, and life skills. When inmates complain about things they cannot do, Gaertner reminds them of all that they can accomplish. After all, people who graduate from Harvard and Yale have limits, too – but those people don't dwell on what they cannot do.

If that sounds a little like coaching, the athletic shoe fits. Gaertner was the point guard on a junior college team from Independence, Kansas, that won a national championship. He coached at the college level, including a stint at Towson University. He coached with the legendary Jim Valvano at Johns Hopkins, the University of Connecticut and Iona. He was the head coach at Norwich University in Vermont.

He was inducted into the New England Basketball Hall of Fame in 2015 in the Pathfinders Category for people with New England roots who left the region and earned great distinction in basketball and/or society. Those coaching skills and basketball connections still pay dividends. Basketball is "the common language" inside prisons.

But faith remains his foundation. He attends Mass regularly and is now an oblate novice at the Benedictine community of St. Anselm's Abbey in Washington, D.C.

"The only way I can say I am sorry to my victim and others I harmed is to wake up every day and do the best (I can) and be the best person I can be that day."

The Prodigal Son, Rembrandt, circa 1667

A prodigal is a person who leaves home and behaves recklessly but later makes a repentant return.

The moral lesson of the Prodigal Son is there is always hope for RESTORATION! This is the story Jesus Christ told in Luke 15. It is also the story of a family's journey to restoration and reconciliation! The father is a symbol of God.

The goal of this workplan is to help you restore your life – your **Business of Living.**

GO FORWARD!

APPENDIX A - BUSINESS OF LIVING COACHING AGREEMENT

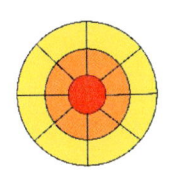

Gatekeepers' mission is to motivate, empower, and encourage inmates and ex-offenders through its **Business of Living Program**. Gatekeepers' coaches will challenge you to make positive choices that will help create your personal re-entry plan. This Coaching Agreement outlines what we are expecting from you and want you to commit to during the time you are in the **Business of Living Program**.

Expectations
1) Open and honest communication.
2) Active contribution to individual and group discussions, including thoughtful feedback.
3) Full participation in all program activities.
4) Consistent and on-time attendance for all classes, meetings, and appointments.
5) Respectful use of everyone's time.
6) At least 24-hour notice before missing a class, meeting, or appointment.
7) Maintaining a positive attitude.
8) Respect and support others in the **Business of Living Program**.

Program Commitments
1) Set up and complete your first appointment with a Coach within two weeks of joining the **Business of Living Program**.
2) Attend scheduled **Business of Living** classes and one Resource Club meeting per week.
3) Attend one coaching meeting per week (as arranged with your Coach).
4) Fill out and complete your Re-Entry Checklist (found in Chapter 11).

I understand and agree to honor the Gatekeepers Expectations and Program Commitments.

_____   _____
Client signature   Date

_____   _____
Printed Name   Telephone

_____   _____
Coach   Date

Made in the USA
Middletown, DE
02 August 2022